# Dear Vulcan

# Dear Vulcan

*Poems*

## Laura Davenport

LOUISIANA STATE UNIVERSITY PRESS

BATON ROUGE

Published by Louisiana State University Press
Copyright © 2020 by Laura Davenport
All rights reserved

LSU Press Paperback Original
First printing

Designer: Laura Roubique Gleason
Typeface: Whitman
Printer and binder: LSI

Library of Congress Cataloging-in-Publication Data

Names: Davenport, Laura, 1984– author.
Title: Dear vulcan : poems / Laura Davenport.
Description: Baton Rouge : Louisiana State University Press, 2020.
Identifiers: LCCN 2019040527 (print) | LCCN 2019040528 (ebook) |
    ISBN 978-0-8071-7073-1 (paperback) | ISBN 978-0-8071-7342-8 (pdf)
    | ISBN 978-0-8071-7343-5 (epub)
Subjects: LCGFT: Poetry.
Classification: LCC PS3604.A94263 D43 2020  (print) | LCC PS3604.
    A94263 (ebook) | DDC 811/.6—dc23
LC record available at https://lccn.loc.gov/2019040527
LC ebook record available at https://lccn.loc.gov/2019040528

The paper in this book meets the guidelines for permanence and
durability of the Committee on Production Guidelines for Book
Longevity of the Council on Library Resources. ∞

For Ben

# Contents

# Dear Vulcan

# The Lisbon Typist

Across the plaza, a woman bursts open,
emerges from her self in a cloud of moths.
Her self is not her self—not *hers*. Down the *ruas*

radiating down the damp back of the city,
lamps are lit. Your lover wants to be another,
different sort of man. He writes to you from other lives—

doctor, sailor, theologian—how the sun sets
over the Indian Ocean. You read his latest tract alone,
fingers pulsing from the early cold, walk home

to the patterned swish of stockings, light pressure
around your thighs. How can you lose the self
when you have a body that burns?

Tonight is the first frost, and in the morning
he will come to you dressed as a poor farmer
with a gift of white asparagus. Or as a mechanic,

wiping his hands. He may come to you
a priest or soldier, poems folded in a pocket,
and you will study this stranger

as he stands on the rug, bewildered
by the newness of his body, as he asks you
for a cup of coffee, a little bit of bread.

# The Year of Small Boats

The motor churns up mud, the tide too low,
the August air heavy with itself,

and you ask if I'm afraid to spend the night
with you, in this johnboat tied to the dock

of a summer house. Off John's Island,
the road ravels back to pine woods

and plantation scars cut through the marsh,
where we explore the roosts of pelicans

and cranes, white smatterings where you find
a small, hollow femur, the kind of omen

you've sought all summer, squinting
behind dark glasses as the dock lifts

with a speedboat's passing, as though
the waving grass and sunlight on the water

pained you, as from the warped gangway
that leads up to the house, I study the line

where mud turns into grass. Because I love you,
I ask straight out: *Is it my mouth, my body*

*that could heal you?* I'll lie down on this oyster bed
where the water laps. You laugh,

say you wish instead to be marooned here
forever, open another beer, not ready to forget her

yet. You tell a joke: *don't listen to men*
*who give advice.* The cooler fills with empties,

and I think of all the people who have given you
empty offers. When you ask, will this feeling

get worse? I want to believe this latest loss
has made a man of you. And when you turn away

to piss, I take in your brown shoulders and the curve
of your calf. You've sworn to remember this

as a year of sorrow, but I will see you balancing
your small craft, giving the finger to the speedboats

as their wakes rock us high against the dock.
Remember, too, the wasp circling your green trunks,

the way we jump into the mud, sink ankle deep.
How brown and slick, like clay, it stains my fingers

as I spread it over my arms, my thighs, your chest,
the pale edge of your collar bone.

# Beach Town in Winter

Through gray glazed meld of sky and water
fading into dusk, we struggled through the wind

toward the bar's lit beacon, collided with a girl
in the doorway. She pressed against us, breath

of whiskey, smile-hissed *faggots*
at our backs. An instant—

the wind forced closed the heavy door,
and she was out. We kept our coats on, ordered

local drafts, in separate silences reviewed
the day just gone: We'd stopped to watch a wedding

on the beach, last of the season—bride
shivering in a thin dress, the groom's coat

stung with wind-whipped sand. Then,
like a blurred-edged dream, that girl

in the doorway—her thin mouth curved
around archaic curses, young face aged

from drink and smoke. When I asked *why?*
My brother shrugged, released her with a breath,

a sip of beer. But she was out there
with her bored and boring hate, is out there still—

malevolent spirit stumbling through the cold,
clear night, the sand and wind.

# On Turkey Creek

The wood-framed bridge, soft
rills underneath,
packed clay at the crossing—

more real than the creek's name
is my father's mouth
shaping it, moustache

like underbrush
sliding under the fenders, thicket
spilling into washed-out road.

I can't account for this memory—
black hulks perched from bank
to bank along the railings, that rotting

bridge with forty buzzards
guarding it. My father had come
to count them,

a tick in his notebook for each
hooked beak. Ahead,
the road bent through laurel

and azalea, a mile or more,
but we never reached that side.
This was the only crossing,

and the bridge would hold
no more unnatural weights.
I kept one hand on the car door

as he paced to the edge and back.
The turkey vultures dozed there
in late sun, bent a shriveled head

to preen, leaves rustling
with riverbed heat, the dry
dirt road. My father tells me

none of this happened,
that it was only the name
of the creek that made me think

dark creatures guarded it,
but when I see them hovering
in summer thermals,

wheeling over the highway,
I remember that stench,
legs scalded with shit

that bleached the rotting boards,
and tell myself that nothing
followed us from there. We left

no trace, no way to find us—
the truck reversed through thicket
to the baked mud road.

We did not cross the threshold.
In that unnerving council,
not a head turned.

# Why We Don't Write about Kudzu

As if it's not enough that the twelve-fifteen
with its mile of coal cars comes to rest
fifty yards from the porch, idling awhile
before it resumes a slow, northward shuffle,

and the halting clank of car meeting car
echoes through our sleep, a line snaking back
along the lip of the river like a slow tune
we cross, re-cross in dreams

as the refinery lights' slow blink powders the room,
and the headlights on the county road
slice through the trees like the brakeman's ghost
still checking the rails as high schoolers parked

in the parallel fields keep watch
for his slow, hovering lamp.
If the night is warm enough and wet,
salamanders cross the dark, slick roadways,

seeking still pools in the ditches,
the shallows beneath a bridge where the lone
dawn heron stands loose and alert,
a spark of aluminum in the reeds.

After years, still new to this place,
you try to give meaning to these visitations,
as if a pine's particular notch
or the sudden shift of sparrows in flight

were blessings, as if blessings were the same
as touch. Once, you felt it, what is whispered
by the highway markers wrapped in weeds.
You were photographing dusty boilers

of the iron works closed since '71,
and you could almost name it
as you paused atop a hill of slag,
rubbed rust from your palms:

an old dog licked the shine from a potato chip bag
and you felt the weight of a hand on your back,
remembered the boy falling into that furnace,
retreating men, the hot ore emptied out

on the ground. The next day,
they had been turned away at the gate,
those same men who watch you in silence
from the bridge, raise their eyes to follow you past—

lazy, afloat on an inner tube, pale skin
and bikini. They hate you, you know,
your bare skin reddening in the light. Still,
you feel chosen, as if the river curls

around you, presses you forward,
and at your passing the woods begin to unfurl
heavy, delicate blossoms: pink lady's
slipper, low stalks of jack-in-the-pulpit gleaming

white through the undergrowth, a telephone pole
enmeshed, great jade vines throttling the wires.

# Damsel, 1990

In the neighbor's damp backyard, I call
the boys stick-fighting on the patio.
The rain steams off the grass. I press clasped
hands into my back until I feel real
chains, the redness that will last
all day. I wait to be rescued, listen
for their footsteps, victors of pretend battle.
These invisible bonds will keep me
in place, black go-go boots,
this invisible zippered jumpsuit.

# Some Women Fling Open Their Shutters

after Cesare Pavese

It's raining on houses: the blind drops roll
down red-tiled roofs, scattering people

and things; hunched under awnings, the children
in their school clothes, the café breaking up,

saucers and papers held high, cups catching rain.
Some women fling open their shutters, pull wash

from the lines. High over the street the pulleys
creak and move. It must be redone, shaken out,

rinsed again and dried, the sky already on its way
to dusk. Now children slither in, soaked,

fling rolled kneesocks on the radiator.
The room is damp and warm, strung-up laundry

tickles their necks. A fan whirs.
Didn't these women see what would happen?

Gathering clothes from corners, under beds,
the morning clouds piled on the sky's edge.

Dark imprints from the first drops dampened undershirts,
twill workpants weighted the line. Day's labor

is gone. No time now to laze under a lamp, warm
in the rising breeze. No time to read husband's paper

and with care recrease, press it smooth
into its place beside his chair.

# In the City without Women

This field is no good, which is why
the horse has wandered. Two men
slap dust from their boots.
All day the boy leans
against the fence, watching the men
and the tiny, purple flowers.

He knows it isn't hard
to catch a horse. At dusk he lies
flat in the field, until his body
is grass. All the sounds of night
grow sharp, then soften.

Now the horse does not
know him. At dawn,
the boy can feel warm breath
in his ear, a wet mouth
searching the flowers.

# Porpoises

In college I spent whole days by the river
watching yachts drift, toward dusk
finding a bench on the white gravel path
to catch the harbor breeze. I filled page
after page in notebooks or sketched the palms
outlined against the sky. And once,
deep in a story I was writing about seeing myself
as a twin—the twin and I were talking—
a man approached in a half-hearted jog
and stopped to say something about the weather.
*Yes,* I said, *it's nice,* and he asked my name
and whether I went to the college. *Yes,* I said.
I did not know what to say to a man that old,
so I pointed to the river, said *look,*
where the sleek fins lifted in rhythm,
my favorite thing about that place
and, still, about those days. Though I could calculate
their speed, the current, where they'd surface
was always a surprise. The man sighed,
and now I am not sure whether he sat or only
stood there, but I believe he sat,
and the sigh was like dropping a heavy load
with the knowledge that soon he would lift it
again. *Actually,* he began, the words far off
as if I had retreated into myself—
*those are porpoises.* I stared ahead as he explained
the size of fins, blowholes, their gray flanks lost
in the dazzle of ripples from a boat.
I couldn't tell you why, even now,
but I am certain they were dolphins
as I was certain then that something had begun—

in airport lounges, polished bars, a corner table—
I would never again be allowed to sit alone
with a book, or keep my own counsel,
or stare off in silence. Either you are nodding now,
or you are shaking your head,
putting down this book to tell me I am wrong,
that no one sees a woman alone
like a coin to pocket, a sunset
to photograph and keep. I don't remember
how I got the man to leave,
unless it was to become so small and still
I blended with the bench, the stones, the water.

# Sermon: New Orleans

Pause with me awhile in this thick, sweet hangover:
a rail straight down the river's back,

brown Mississippi stinking in August heat.
Our streetcar whines along the track,

passes its twin: green-gold car
packed with tourists, cameras held high

to capture light. Our stale breath
flowers the glass.

———

Call this the present:
the car is too full

yet the driver keeps stopping,
pulls the great lever, collects more fares.

The heat condenses between our bodies.
I search for Jamie

in the sun's slant through the window,
in figures which turn at the light,

dip through blurred lines of crosswalk,
stripes winnowed to cigarettes,

one burning, always,
in his mouth.

Because I never learned where he was buried,
each corridor of alley light we pass

shares the burden of his body, marked by gardens
glimpsed through thickening shade, strange

statuettes, walls overwrought with flowers.
I lived out the year of his death encased

in the scent of jasmine, walked home
through the night-thick air

from the apartment of one man or another.
Once, still flushed and certain of my body,

I lay down on the sun-warmed bricks
beneath the layered limbs of an oak

and tried to feel what death meant.
It was autumn, late. No cars passed.

I listened to the distant trains, believed it all
erasable: Jamie, always nervous,

the black marks of the hanging moss
shadowing my throat, the humid air

torn inland from the marsh, pale lights,
and what he saw: crush of neon,

hurricane glasses, lit sign over the bar
he might have been to that night,

fingers laced in public with another boy
for the first time. The car and unknown driver,

corner rounded too fast—curb, mailbox,
boys again.

———————

You may figure no one is keeping track
of our losses—

the trolley lurches
toward the Quarter,

steel box we'll leap from, gasping.
No memory, later,

of these trials.
The bruised river will stretch on,

powdered sugar will lace
our tongues

like the white marches
of the paddle boats,

the great wheels catching debris.
Like us,

he is nowhere in particular now.

———

I can convince you we were close,
he and I, through detail:

We were born in the same
town. I tell you of the Christmas

I saw him in a basement, and he showed me
his first boyfriend's photo,

pressed in his wallet. How long
did I stare at that picture?

Or did I glance and murmur,
look away? What I wanted to say

was a burr on my tongue. It was snow
in my throat. I know heat:

shoulder blades flexing
beneath your hands. He couldn't wait

to get back to the crumbling student houses,
the bars on Freret street, fallen porches

we pass now as driveways spindle out
through manicured lawns.

Because he felt free there, because
they couldn't stop kissing.

———

You will have to forgive the punchline,
the story we all repeated: his grandmother

in pearls and black, down from Alabama,
carving a ham after the funeral.

A troupe of earringed boys lined up with plates.

———

That summer I came upon a whitewashed church
alone in the woods—

pines grew into the walls,
but the paint, in the overcast light, still glowed

and the truth at times is like those heavy doors
I was afraid to touch. To understand,

you have to go back, forget
what you know. Not white, that church,

from holiness but from a perpetual
trust. Men came each month to trim

encroaching vines. The water later
covered it—pulled pews into the nave

as if to make room for a dance,
or Wednesday supper. The hurricane erased, too,

tire marks and glass, the park
where Jamie sat and smoked in afternoons.

Or didn't sit. I never really knew him.
But I heard the friends drove overnight

up the coast to see his body. Polite distance
a clearing between them and the family.

Their clothes: garish orange and pink,
tall boots scuffed the linoleum. So the grandmother

picked up a diamond stud one of the boys
had lost, gave it back. Who makes a moral out of that?

# In the City without Women

In terms of stones,
it takes a day to cross
from one end of the known

world to the other:
starting at the biggest boulder
in the farthest field,
past the plow-churned giants
by the road. Past scattered

concrete bits between the shops,
and the strange, small,
pinkish ones

that wash up by the river,
smooth stones the boy pockets
as he walks,
scanning the ground for another.

# Black and White of James Dean

In what would be green lawn, he holds
a gray leaf, cross-
legged, counting the poplar's
small veins, dark
threads, each line in his face
drawn down. It appears to be
spring, the moment private.
Still, a camera catches his costar
reclining beside him,
dark hair swept back
from her face: Liz Taylor, beaming,
watches and smokes,
the space between them lit,
exposure whitening
the grass. As if to say
celebrities, too, count
blossoms, he frowns at the lawn.
His cuffs are pressed, his collar curves
beautifully, closed over his chest
with a dark button.
These days, fresh deaths
eclipse each other at newer,
better angles: by fire, water, speed,
held-down desires.
In the still afternoon, a break
between takes, what do you say
to her? Tell a joke, aware of the lens,
devise, perhaps, an escape?
Do you wish
for a smaller soul, one the world
will not be sore at you

for taking back?
This is the set of your last
film, and, watching now,
you look so tired, Jim.
But I do not think you know that.
Rather than write out
who will receive each piece
of you, your wristwatch, gold-plated
lighter, you are thinking
about leaves—what kind are they?
Why have you never studied them?

# You Choose to Dream of Fishing

How long do you sit in the dark
or light room, waiting for your name
to be called? When do you realize
no one is coming? Rise, then,
and walk through this quiet depot.

Inside infinity, you choose to dream
of fishing. If you must be stuck, let it be
on the clearest day. So it appears:
the little boat you sanded and painted
is balanced on a lake, grass tall around the shore.

The line unspools. From the past
you no longer have, memories threaten:
walking home in the dark, the pavement
hurtling up, the hem of your blue shirt,
tilting street, your hand on the ground.

Here, the sun is stuck at twelve o'clock.
Waves lap like your mother's palms
smoothing a blanket. You cast, reel in, cast.
The water is dark below you. Far off, a splash.

# The Susans

Three days ago, in a darkened house,
your mother and my mother sipped pinot grigio,

knit small blankets, called late asking *are you
awake? I've made a painting*

*even you will like.* It would have been your birthday,
so your mother and my mother watched

romantic comedies, took turns evading
questions, possibly ate ice cream. Forgive me,

when I grumbled into the phone *What painting? Where?*
I didn't know our photo was on the mantle there

and my mother had her thumb on the frame,
apologized for smudging the silver.

When you died or were killed or passed on,
when your grandmother held my wrists

in the church basement filled with high school
boyfriends, and trapped my hands

between her cold, dry palms, I couldn't go back—
the books I loaned you packed up

with the rest of your things. Now the Susans take turns
clipping recipes, send them to my out-of-state-address.

They join clubs (books, photography), experiment
with bangs. Each week in swim class,

in the shallow pool they wave their arms,
backstroke in black ruffled suits.

You'd want to know your mother learned
the breaststroke, crawling through the water,

cheeks flushed from treading in place,
and she enjoys the trails her fingers carve,

her true weight revealed by the volume
displaced, a grief she climbs into,

lifting her up as it pulls her back down.

# Vista

We share a burger,
what he could afford,
in silence watch a troop of ants
ravage a crinkle fry
in the Baptist parking lot
where lovers go—above the hospital
and decommissioned blast
furnace, the best free view
in town. An hour before,
he'd shuffled atop me,
hands splayed as if climbing
a mountain. I watch him
lick fine salt dust
from his thumbs.
It will be years before I learn
this easy fact:
a lot of things are not contained
in rock and roll.
Like what to do
when that levee runs dry,
when to let a man
save face, and how
to let my anger simmer,
stoic as a blue gas flame,
so it stays lit for years
feeding on air.

# Boys of 2001

In that summer's hit song, I imagined myself
the woman in the white convertible: downshifting

at the crosswalk as young boys discovered hope,
would say aloud years later, *If I ever saw her again . . .*

There were the rambling neighborhood night walks,
homecoming banners, shadow circles printed by porch lights

on a lapel. What makes me think again, today,
of the wind combing dark trees, the memories of those boys

like the shadows of limbs outside my window? In this city
they will never see, through old leaves swept off

from the glistening, still road, all winter I've recited
this litany: names misremembered, found again,

peeked through fences at the dry, shaded gardens
until I almost see their budding, stubbled faces—

John standing in a rain-soaked driveway, Steven
on the canyon drive, and Anthony, and Chris, and Dan, and on—

I can't stop speaking to these boys, married now,
or gone, telling their stories back to them, revising

until they blur and I remember them mostly
by the cars they owned: red Saab convertible, the rusted Volvo

that never ran, my favorite blue Honda that may still
sit empty, in the wide church lot, under a pine.

# In the City without Women

The boy says, someday I will see the ocean
and it will move me. He sits in the lane
in the expanding dusk, his back
against the wall of a house.

The boy has learned words from a sailor's book:
whitecap, trough. When you walk
in the salty water, the cuts on your ankles
will sting.

The boy wants only to sit on a wall
with his feet in the sand. To watch men
cast lines into the waves
and smell the wind.

Really, the boy is afraid. He has heard
about the tides—the way, at night,
the sea draws forward,
as if of its own accord.

# In a Nashville Liquor Store, I Realize I Don't Love You

Outside, late snowflakes
fleck the car, reflect
the red-green strands of tinsel
left over from the holiday.
Three days after New Year's,
we are buying champagne.
I watch you pull stiff
twenties from a pocket,
the cash you made tonight,
enough for a bottle
and six-pack, enough
to drink ourselves to sleep.
We've come from a party
where the room unspooled,
a girl collapsed on a sofa
gripping a fifth of whiskey,
skirt hiked up around her thighs,
exposing fine hairs, dark cotton
panties. You collect change,
your shadow in the window flickers
with fluorescents over the aisles
of mixers, rum and vodka,
jewel-like bottles of gin, the TV
monitor the clerk, briefly,
glances from. The crowd pressed in
around the girl, then, bored,
moved off to other rooms.
I watched you pass a smoke
among the boys and felt your hand
span the back of my neck,
jugular to jugular, the pressure

a hot buzz in my ears. I need
to tell you, as you gather up the booze,
hold open the door, pause
to light a smoke below the flashing OPEN
sign, there are things I can never
forgive: the blonde wisps
on her thighs, your slow nod
as if to say she deserves whatever happens
next. I thought she sickened me,
but I was afraid to touch her:
roll together her soft thighs,
gather that bunched fabric in my hands,
to smooth the crumpled hem.

# Notes from My Other Life

Some fictitious village burns
on the page, defeated Persians
huddle and Pessoa describes
their dying: the wall scaled,
ever off-screen women pinned
against it. It's hopeless, but then
the second author intervenes,
the girl who owned this book
forgotten semesters ago.
In bubbly, rounded pen she gives back
the meaning of events:
trees ripe with *structured emptiness,*
leaves afire in the summer air
release acrid *aesthetic purity*
which cloaks the ancient men
who sit and smoke, *indifferent*
to the screams of women dragged
from the wombs of their homes
into the world, into the burning air
of *modernity.* The readers—she and I—
sit through the lecture as the old men,
waiting out the siege, play endless
chess. And where the poem ends,
her pen creates
bold loops around the margins
as the invaders, finished with the women,
hack at the old men:
*I am so happy I am so*
*happy I am a kappa*
*kappa kappa kappa gamma.*

# Lessons from a Normal Childhood

I may have dreamed the preschool on a hill
above the hospital, how the staff
who did not at the time seem bored but seemed

to cherish us released us to the yard to watch
the medevac touch down—a treat,
the shocking noise, because we knew no

injury, and it was too far distant to make out
small figures on the gurneys. And because
my mother worked there, at the hospital,

I told myself she must be among the white coats
rushing to meet the blades, and cheered her
because I believed she could hear me and knew,

somehow, she needed it. Years later,
over dinner, with her back to the television,
she told me pointed stories about teenage mothers,

how small their babies were, the fathers
had no teeth left—although the chance
I'd end up doing meth was slim, or even that I'd learn

where to find it, since you can only ever tell
after the fact, after the shit goes up in flames,
after the whole mess blows—

then you can see beside some country road
the charred halves of a mobile home, the burn so new
the kudzu has not yet begun to cover it.

# Sand Dollar

It was the devil in me,
when she came home with a sand dollar
tattoo, a life-sized gray-green blob
on her shoulder blade
that would not give me anything
worth saying.

That devil, as I see it, fills me up,
like the Mason jar vases she kept
on the window sills. It made me laugh
and touch her boyfriend's hand.
It made me crank the volume up

then turn it down, the house so quiet
I could hear her crouched
in the turn of the stair, her caught breath
begging me to do it,
she and the devil both,
to prove them right.

# Aubade: Evidence

Last night, a little drunk, you bragged about sex
in cars—awoke with his name

on the roof of your mouth, first light
recalling the body's questions, the milky glare

through the windshield as taillights wound red
trails behind you, that old city staring back.

You had laughed, detailing his car, his clothes,
dark corners of the parking deck, and the rub of denim

on skin, as though you hadn't just laid bare the last,
small secret—some mornings you wake feeling haunted,

hear voices in the kettle steam. *Relax, relax,*
That urging heard many times since then, insistence

first timid, then not—his keys swayed in the ignition
and you can't remember saying *yes,* or *no.*

He's nothing now except that part of you that says
it never happened, then, it did, the girl

still being driven home along the cliff road,
gazing down into the yards of girls just like you,

studying his hands on the wheel, their sudden gentleness
resting there, so that years later it is only his hands

that come back, and the chime of your key
missing the front door lock, undressing alone in your room,

pale wrists turned to the mirror to catch
the fading heat of him, the proof already gone.

# Local Attraction

The bear will not come down—claws clamped
around the pine's trunk, the one tree thick enough
to hold him, a nest of grackles in the first high branch.
He scratches at the bark, and to his sinking weight
a keeper on the ground shouts *here, bear!*
Her voice melts into air. The park is closing.
Ravenous, blank-eyed goats retire to straw beds,
sheep slow their grazing, and on the far edge
white-tailed deer fade back into the man-made thicket.
But the children with fingers wound through the chain-link
barrier refuse to leave, will wait
until the bear comes down. We watch
them watch the keeper call, again and again. I reach
for your hand, craving that breath of skin to skin,
the way geese settle on a lake, find only air—
you've wandered, blending with the scene,
all those tilted necks in the falling light.
The bear looks down, tree wrapped in an embrace,
unable to climb higher, unwilling to descend.
The keeper offers steak, a raw red brick
held level in her outstretched hands.

# In the City without Women

Across the river, mown fields gather
light. The boy asks, who owns a wall?
The man who pulls stones from the field,
the man who shapes them? He drops a twig
into the river. What a man can enclose

is his. The boy extends his arms, raises
the tips of his fingers
like the dancer on the poster outside the theater,
like when he was smaller,
and he noticed the small, brown birds.

He likes to stand on high things
and look down, and watch the water
rise. Far off, it's raining hard.
Someday he'll see these hills
rinsed free of green.

# Dear Vulcan

The world's largest cast-iron statue, *Vulcan* is the symbol of Birmingham,
Alabama, and stands atop Red Mountain overlooking the city.

Deity of retraced steps, observe these hands:
again they grip the wheel,

car parked beside a rain-wet mailbox,
dark house of another old flame

whose father planned a quick sale,
cheap move north. The house stays vacant,

third yard on this block gone
to seed. Above the grass, hanging limp

in the half-light, a realtor's sign sways—
a woman's face stares out through plastic

gloss. My mother's house was an uphill walk
from here, and the same woman sold it.

I had drawn an X across her photograph
for a look she gave my father, unhooked

her hanging sign, and threw it away.
This was before I tried to name

the texture of the light outside these windows,
the pattern maple leaves made

on the driveway. And still I drive in circles,
looking for a quiet spot. The question is

what keeps me coming back:
this cul-de-sac of black-windowed houses,

this god who, again and again,
shows me only his shoulder.

# Reconsider the Western

How the whore stands wordless on the balcony,
her window one light in a black well, the alley
where the hero's bobbing Stetson disappears—

the hat he crushed or twirled
between his hands as he sat dumbstruck
on the bed. Not taking her, no, but having

been moved, he left a few coins
anyway. Easy sex must have impediments—
buck teeth or scars, a child tucked away

who is, in the end, revealed—some outward
semblance of shame. But this one: she's frail,
consumptive, the pitiful ward

of the madam, and the hundreds of men
that pass through the territory
are like clouds passing over the still plain

of her body, the field our hero stumbles onto,
drunk on whiskey and the morning glow,
wheat colored like her hair.

It's like this: afraid, but drawn to her,
he wants her but not here, not now.
As he rides past the double-forked cottonwood,

a branch bends to the water as she is bending,
dips fresh cloth to wipe the dust of travel
from each new face, each rough and heavy customer.

# When You Talk about Old Girlfriends

You could say *biggest mahi ever*—
of the glazed-over eye slapped up
below the sign for half-day charters,

this afternoon's catch nailed
to the plywood marquee—could say,
as I snag a sip of your beer, as couples

with Long Islands pose below the hanging fins,
*that reminds me.* If I needed to know,
I'd have read somewhere

that the most perfect skin tones
are olive; her eyes were almond shaped
and so clear I am forced to imagine

seawater splooshing against pylons,
the gentle rocking wakes as the charter boats idle,
unload unused bait.

I think, *you look so beautiful,* get the usual:
a chuckle, an elbow urging me closer
to the stand, those bright ruby droplets

studding a gill. *Oh look,* I say,
two jays are pestering a crow, careening
in soft, ever-tightening loops.

Gulls circle as ever in the rough wind,
eying the fish—poor bastards
that take whatever they can get.

# Pool Hall

Third round, the topic turns to skin:
in the Hilton corridor, he says, the girl tried

to say goodnight, goodbye, confessed
her mother was asleep in the next room.

He took her in the hallway
by the ice machine. The storyteller racks

the balls, breaks, proceeds to the next setup,
and she is too aware of her warm,

small breasts, her ass, the distance from here
to the car. If Hell exists for certain,

it's this basement pool hall, beers
sweating on the table and men circling

under the lights. And if it's Hell, what had she done?
Now fiddling with her phone, condemned

to watch them line up shots, eternally
sitting it out. Condemned to never touch the cue

without their hands on her hips, a game
you cannot ever win if you can't lean

over the table. She must have been, in life,
one of them—muscled, tanned, quick to order

drinks or offer directions—because she feels
that other life fully, and she is back there

in that Hilton hallway, confusing love
for a muffled gasp, a push for a pull,

the air compressors kicking on,
a cold blast rattling her spine.

# If, after I Die, They Want to Write My Biography

after Fernando Pessoa

Tell them I had an excellent ear.
Do not say I deceived you.
When they wish you to describe
my likes, my habits, well,

some things are personal.
Show off: well-tuned guitar,
shoes lined with mates, extensive
alphabetized library (providing
I have done these things).

Say I have not passed on, rather
drifted off, as on a ship I loved
or conversation. Then play
all twenty-seven
mixtapes you made
because you can't stop grieving,
spend nights counting off
the quiet beats between songs,

the click of the rewind.
When you wake cold, remember:
I miss you most. Don't think
otherwise. Beg me to haunt you.

Beg my pregnant ghost, round,
open mouth. Tell them I am
wherever you are now.

# Quitting

Every cigarette I smoked was sorrowful and so
I gave them up. I didn't inhale, had to lean
against a porch rail
with one floodlight behind me
and the yard below had to be dark.
In the car I was afraid
the ash would set aflame the back seat,
the fire would spread to the gas tank
and the open bottles
of Zima. And the shame of drinking Zima
stays with me whenever I hear that song
we played which meant everything
as if our lives could be summed up, just like that,
beautiful and full of longing.
Could be charted, verse and chorus,
like the staggered tarot lines we read the future in,
a few short weeks in summer.
Had I known I would not miss them,
the boys whose faces I traced in sleep
and in the day could not raise my eyes to,
I would have asked the cards
something else: What will I say to my daughter
of memory? That it is like the bright nail
I picked up in the street, carried for a block
and hid, out of sight, in the sewage drain
and this gutter is not the one
I floated boats in, and the boats you will make
from paper are not like mine
at all. And there will be a woman
or man someday you would like to forget
existed, and you will be alone then,

the last one riding in the car at night.
It's easy—all you have to do:
don't listen to that song again.
And once you are alone in the dark
you must not lean into it.

# Apology for a Horse

I won't compare us to the ruined horse,
its lifted leg, limp hoof swaying—

though at the time I thought of it.
Admit it, the image is attractive,

like your sun-browned hands on the wheel
as you turned into the unlit station,

walked off to clear your head. Alone
in the dark front seat, it was as if

the soft lawn spread again, green
beneath the clustered blue awnings

baked in June sun, the crowd pressed
close to the fences and the pressed track

hidden from view so that the riders grew larger
with the sound of hooves, obscured

as they passed by women in print dresses
shifting platters to make room for more

cold ham and drumsticks on the folding tables.
Like a girl waiting for directions,

the gray horse halted at the last
turn, hind leg delicately bent.

The jockey dismounted, loosely held the reins
while the other riders paced at the finish, slowed

their mounts. At first the horse looked fine,
even beautiful, and I thought it might walk

the rest of the lap—as though it had forgotten,
mid-race, where it was going, what the hurry

was. Its gray flank shimmered like water
over stones as the ambulance rolled up

and the gathering ring of men tightened.
Then the horse stepped backward

and its leg gave way, shank split
below the knee, the flesh unhinged

and awkward, swaying from the hoof's weight
that couldn't touch down. The crowd's

monotonous chatter stilled, the men bent
to the task. That bit of flesh looked nothing

like a leg. A horse is animal, you said, but part
machine, and I know how bone can splinter

below the skin, some breaks unfair, unmendable.
But I did not know better than to pity us:

drunk, sniveling into your shirt,
my pretty party dress stained, that horse

that wanted only to keep standing.
All evidence removed, the men dispersed

to reveal the warm, even lawn. Another race began.
I could not watch any more, and in the car

you pulled off the road at dusk to find
your bearings. I asked, how was it done?

What kind of trailer did they drag the dead
horse to? Or did they hoist it up

under the belly's hard balloon? Or press down
as it fell onto a flatbed, poison

weaving through its giant heart? I thought
there'd be a gunshot, sudden, echoing

over the track like something from a film.
They used a bolt, you said—

then touched my forehead where the metal
would enter, just shy of the hairline.

You believed I wanted to know
the answer. The calm pressure

of your finger echoed above my eyes
as through the windshield I watched you

methodically wiping the glass. Your face
through soapy film, first blurred, then clear—

four even strokes across, across,
and then a long stroke back.

# Azalea

Too bright to think of lovers
in their boyhood beds, to read *eyes closed*
*you turn to me*

               *I stroke your sleeping*
*face;* this morning I would rather thumb
a gardening book than poetry.

I know it's not magnolia
in the corner of the yard, but find no picture
of the miniature buds burst forth

a week ago, long after dogwood
and crepe myrtle, when I had given the tree up
for dead after the long winter

when the limbs hung choked
with caterpillar gauze. I'd like to be a woman
who weeds and spends each Sunday

on her knees, edging for appearances' sake,
but more often sit tanning with a book
above these tangled beds.

The branches are still bare,
the newly built nests exposed
while the azaleas, already peaked

and color packed, riot at every roadside
without tending. To touch a sleeper's face
is selfish. And those lines below the not-oak

rising up in the morning glare
call back the many boys who, in the dark,
caressed a lip or cheek with all the slowness

of a root edging in earth. And I,
of patience infinite,
kept eyes shut tight or sighed, allowed

whatever pleasure they siphoned
undisturbed, whatever it was they wanted.

# In the City without Women

The boy doesn't know
there are places the stars don't honeycomb
the sky in veils so numerous you cease
to notice them. Still there's this

impulse, like a trace of wood smoke—
the smell of a good fire somewhere
that warms him as he walks, grows
fainter with each turn.

                Sometimes,
the light on his street, his front door,
makes him want to forget
what's inside. But it will be the same
three steps, the hall, whatever shoes
or cup he left, right where he left them.

# Winter Storm

Because the look of drifting snow
burnished by street lamps made us think
of buried cabins, isolated counties

where winter lies heaviest, shivering
in each other's arms we lay with the curtains
open, watching flakes fall,

and I woke to the drone of a plow,
shovels scraping footprints from the walk,
men conversing in soft Spanish

as they cleared the courtyard
between condos. I listened to their breath,
muffled steps around the porch

as they whisked ice from the stairs, and, naked,
went to the window, wrapped
the thin curtain around my body, peered

at their bent backs. Called in at midnight
when the snow stopped falling
to shovel out the condo owners' cars,

they sweated through the freezing night
to leave the world as it was yesterday.
It felt like rescue. In bed, you turned

and hummed a little in your sleep,
a tune you wouldn't remember
that arose from nowhere, drifting

through your mind like this restless
wondering I get at night—the too-bright snow
and men's shadows over it,

carving out a path for us to follow.
I almost woke you then to ask
what shape this love will take, how long

it can last. I let you sleep.
And I am not writing this to ask you
now, but so that I can keep this

question—not a diary, but like the notes
of first explorers, crossing
the wide continent, land new only

to themselves. At night by the fire,
retracing routes and encampments, the map
ever widening, *ocean in view.*

# Request for Patience

Documents burn on the capitol lawn,
and the fields are green around Richmond: 1865,

war ends as light softens husked warehouses,
pavement blushed with April pollen

while a man stands close to the river,
the bridge he crossed burned away. Worn through

and wet, he smells of mold and blood, the sodden
trunks of cherry trees here, on the cemetery ridge

above the fall line. Here, where I am trying
this moment to tell you how the grandfather

of my grandfather turned away from that city's shell,
walked home. Again south, land blooms overnight,

the lane he walks weaving through maple, turkey oak,
and pine, burnt fields and encampments.

In Georgia, he buries the last of his things
and wakes to the slow lilt of bees—his wife

waiting still, recording each new ruin,
fields left to the encroaching woods.

Now picture the warm stripe of sun on his back
(my hand is on your back), the sudden rains

pulled over the hills. I do not know how long it takes
to walk that far, how it feels to wait out midday

in the shade of an oak, dust covering the worn wool
you expected to die in. Who cares whether all this

is true? You want me to say he made it,
didn't lose himself in the play of light, or lean

against a trunk (as I would do), entranced
by the quiet. But isn't there something marvelous

about this waiting? His wife on the porch, shading
her eyes. The slow turn of a day. The space

between what was and what comes after,
which is never empty, but full of our own breath,

the call of mockingbirds. Then I say have patience,
have patience with me. Pretend I am that man walking.

# August Storm at Midnight

Thunder or a premonition woke me—
the world washed away and I should bear

witness: blue flashes in the predawn hour,
rainfall on the roof like the all-consuming static

of recorded dreams. In sleep I had wandered
with you some antebellum halls, and out the giant

louvered windows, rain fell. We were afraid,
in that grand house, to open long-shut doors,

make it ours. The sky this morning was blue,
rinsed of clouds. The night storm washed away

summer's metallic edge from the air.
How long has it been since I found it useful

to describe the sky, clouds knitting over
the long bridge across the marsh, apex

driving us into a net of white? If everything
that can be said, has, then why

that night storm, why this sky?

# Still Life: Master Bedroom

Freeze this tableau: newspapers spread on the floor,
the sun through the east window. An old sheet
drapes the headboard. No drop cloth or tape, paint cans

pried open with the end of a screwdriver. Preserve it,
before I enter all trembling caution, climb the kitchen chair,
reach for the edge where wall meets ceiling. Something lives

in my hands. When I tell them *grip*, they think *drop. Hold*
becomes *shove*, that death wish when the body leans
over a roof's edge, feet urge the legs to step out

into space. How does my husband push the roller up and back
in even strokes, hum something from the radio, spill not one
mint-green drop on the baseboard? How will he later

slide into bed and pull me to his side in one deft motion,
the smell of paint still on our skin, walls moist to the touch?
When I most want to love someone I fear that small, heavy thing

pinballing inside me—these hands now unscrewing a light cover,
an inch from the socket, now reaching out and over to mark
one wavering line of green and then another and another.

# In the City without Women

The boy draws sails with a chip
of stone. This is the ship
he'll build one day. The street
is empty after rain. No sign
of the old dog the boy would like
to catch. He'd brush its fur
and bathe it in the river.

Think hard enough about a thing,
and it happens. The dog
passed through this alley once,
right where the boy is standing.

The boy stretched out his arm
and raked thick fur
with his fingers. The smell stayed
with him the whole day after,
like crushed grass beside the river,
like waking in wet clover.

# Acknowledgments

Many thanks to the editors of the journals, anthology, and magazines in which these poems originally appeared, sometimes in different forms:

*Best New Poets 2009:* "Why We Don't Write about Kudzu"; *Birmingham Arts Journal:* "Winter Storm"; *Boxcar Poetry Review:* "The Susans" and "Boys of 2001"; *Breakwater Review:* "The Lisbon Typist"; *Cider Press Review:* "Porpoises"; *Connotation Press: An Online Artifact:* "The Year of Small Boats," "Request for Patience," and "If, after I Die, They Want to Write My Biography"; *Crab Orchard Review,* "Local Attraction"; *The Delaware Poetry Review:* "Notes from My Other Life," "Aubade: Evidence," "Reconsider the Western," and "Some Women Fling Open Their Shutters"; *The Helen Burns Anthology: Academy of American Poets University and College Prize, 1999–2009:* "Black and White of James Dean"; *The Meadowland Review:* "Azalea"; *Meridian:* "Apology for a Horse"; *New South:* "When You Talk about Old Girlfriends"; *One:* "Quitting"; *Richmond Magazine:* "Sermon: New Orleans"; *The Sow's Ear Poetry Review:* "On Turkey Creek"; *Synaesthesia Magazine:* "In a City without Women" ("This field is no good"), "In a City without Women" ("In terms of stones"), "In a City without Women" ("The boy says"), "In a City without Women" ("The boy doesn't know"), and "In a City without Women" ("The boy draws sails"); *Tinderbox Poetry Journal:* "In a Nashville Liquor Store, I Realize I Don't Love You," "Lessons from a Normal Childhood," and "Vista."

# Notes

The title "Some Women Fling Open Their Shutters" comes from a line in Cesare Pavese's poem "Tolerance" in *Disaffections: Complete Poems 1930–1950*, trans. Geoffrey Brock (Port Townsend, WA: Copper Canyon Press, 2002).

"Notes from My Other Life" references Fernando Pessoa's poem "I heard it told that once in Persia" in *Poems of Fernando Pessoa*, trans. Edwin Honig (San Francisco: City Lights Publishers, 2001).

"If, after I Die, They Want to Write My Biography," is inspired by Fernando Pessoa's poem "If, After I Die, They Should Want to Write My Biography" in *Poems of Fernando Pessoa*, trans. Edwin Honig (San Francisco: City Lights Publishers, 2001).

Italicized lines in "Azalea" are from David Wojahn's poem "Napping on My 53rd Birthday" in *Interrogation Palace* (University of Pittsburgh Press, 2006).

The last line of "Winter Storm" references the journal of William Clark of the famed Lewis and Clark Expedition, wherein the explorer expresses confidence that his Corps of Discovery team had reached the end of its journey. (It hadn't.)